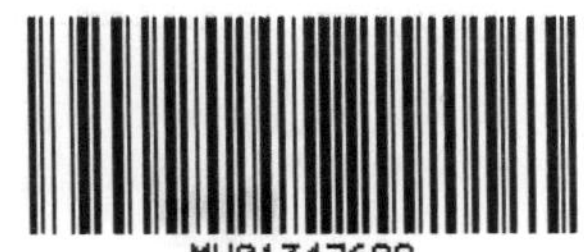

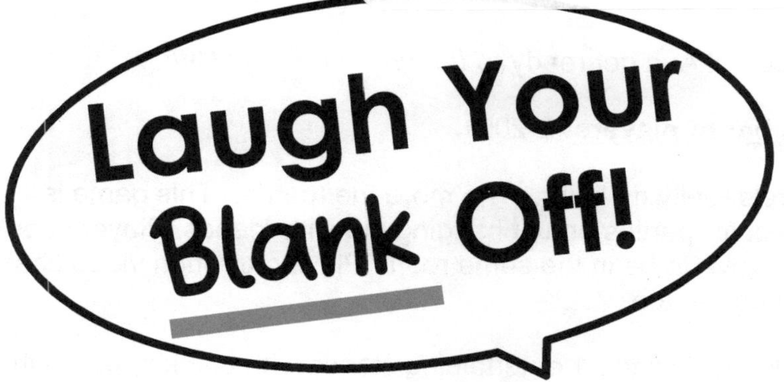

Ad Libs for Adults 😂

Travel Edition

JBC Story Press

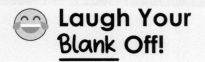

Welcome! And get ready to *Laugh Your Blank Off!*

Number of players: 2-200+

There's really no limit… The more the merrier! This game is perfect for parties or just hanging out with friends. Players don't even have to be in the same room. Playing through video chat works great too.

Inside, you'll find 21 entertaining stories with blank spaces where words have been left out. Each story comes with a list of missing words of various types, e.g., ADJECTIVE, ADVERB, NOUN, EXCLAMATION, etc.

For each story, one player is the Story Teller. The Story Teller asks the other players to call out words to fill in the spaces of the story — WITHOUT first telling them what the story is about.

And bam! Just like that, you have a RIDICULOUSLY funny story!

The Story Teller reads the completed story out loud, and you all laugh so hard you almost pee your pants, cry, roll on the floor, or all of the above! *YOU* fill in the blank!

Adult Themes

This version of the game is for "grownups." That means stories may contain references to alcohol, romance, and other crazy adult stuff (you know, like work or parenting). Whether stories include "adult" language is up to you! Some groups like to use "spicy" swear words. Others prefer "sweet" and swear-free. It's your call!

One thing's for sure. Every story you create will be RIDICULOUSLY funny!

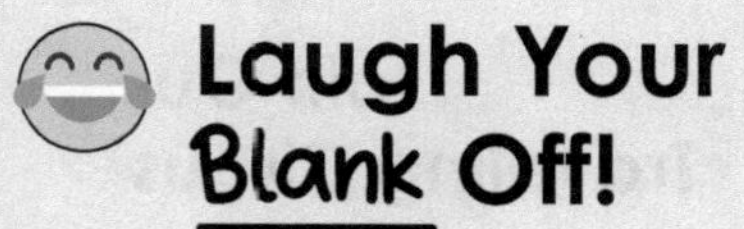

Examples

Before, with blanks:

"_____________ (EXCLAMATION)! We need to _____________ (VERB) to the party as _____________ (ADVERB ENDING IN "LY") as possible. We only have ______ (NUMBER) minutes to get there." So we jumped in the _____________ (ADJECTIVE) car and sped off.

After the Story Teller fills in the blanks with words from the players:

"____Yuck____ (EXCLAMATION)! We need to ____dance____ (VERB) to the party as ____quietly____ (ADVERB ENDING IN "LY") as possible. We only have __900__ (NUMBER) minutes to get there." So we jumped in the ___furry____ (ADJECTIVE) car and sped off.

Quick Review

ADJECTIVE – Describes something or someone. Examples: Funny, huge, bossy, lame, fast.

ADVERB – Describes how something is done. You will only be asked for adverbs that end in "ly." Examples: Happily, badly, loudly.

NOUN or PLURAL NOUN – A person, place or thing. Examples: Singular – sister, book, foot. Plural – sisters, books, feet.

VERB, VERB ENDING IN "ING" or VERB (PAST TENSE) – Verbs are action words. Examples: Verb – Run, kiss, sing; Verb ending in "ing"– running, kissing, singing; Verb (past tense) – ran, kissed, sang

EXCLAMATION – A sound, word, or phrase that is spoken suddenly or loudly and expresses emotions, like excitement or anger, or shock or pain. Examples: "Oh no!", "Awesome!", "You're kidding me!", "Oof!"

OTHER – Specific words, like ANIMAL, BODY PART, CITY, COLOR, FIRST NAME (FRIEND)

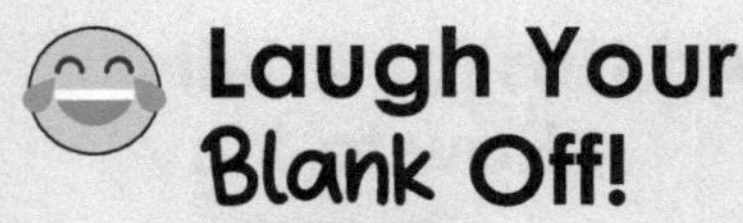

Join Our Traveling Circus

ADJECTIVE
LAST NAME (ANYONE)
NUMBER
NUMBER
ANIMAL (PLURAL)
VERB
COUNTRY
COUNTRY
COUNTRY
VERB ENDING IN “ING”
NOUN
NOUN
TYPE OF SPORT
PLURAL NOUN
PLURAL NOUN
NUMBER
NOUN
ADJECTIVE

Join Our Traveling Circus

Are you looking for a(n) ____________ (ADJECTIVE) job and love to travel? We're The ____________ (LAST NAME (ANYONE)) Family, and we're looking for a nanny to join our traveling circus! With ____________ (NUMBER) kids and ______ (NUMBER) pet ____________ (ANIMAL (PLURAL)), our family is a circus in itself. But we also ____________ (VERB) in a real circus that travels around the world! We need a nanny to join us for an international tour. If you have ever wanted to visit ____________ (COUNTRY), ____________ (COUNTRY), or ____________ (COUNTRY), this is your golden opportunity! As our ____________ (VERB ENDING IN "ING") nanny, your duties will include helping the kids get ready each morning, supervising their ____________ (NOUN) work, serving meals, and putting them to ____________ (NOUN) at night. You must also love to have fun! We need a nanny who enjoys ____________ (TYPE OF SPORT), playing board ____________ (PLURAL NOUN), sightseeing, and laughing at silly ____________ (PLURAL NOUN). You will get two days off per week and compensation is $____________ (NUMBER) for the full tour. To apply, please record a ____________ (NOUN) of yourself sharing your work experience and some of your ____________ (ADJECTIVE) hobbies. We look forward to hearing from you!

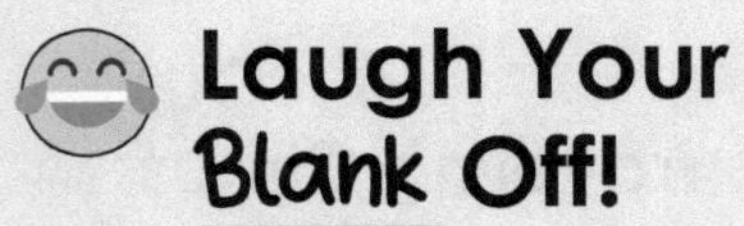

NOUN
PLURAL NOUN
VERB (PAST TENSE)
EUROPEAN CITY
EMOTION
VERB ENDING IN “ING”
FOOD
BEVERAGE
OCCUPATION
EUROPEAN CITY
EXCLAMATION
VERB (PAST TENSE)
ADJECTIVE
NOUN
EMOTION
VERB ENDING IN “ING”
FOOD
BEVERAGE

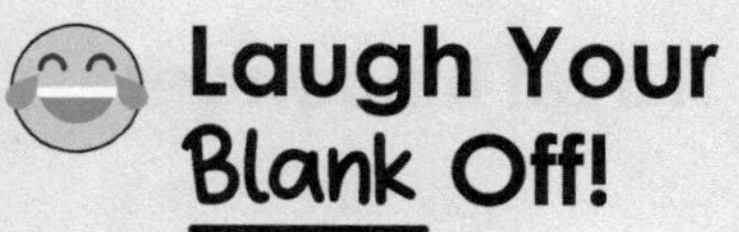

Destination Unknown

You've heard the advice, "look before you leap." Now, here's a story about why you should also look before you sleep! When I was a ____________ (NOUN) student, I took a trip to Europe with my ____________ (PLURAL NOUN). We bought Eurail passes and ____________ (VERB (PAST TENSE)) on an overnight train in Amsterdam. Our plan was to wake up in ____________ (EUROPEAN CITY) the next day. We were ____________ (EMOTION) to explore the city, go ____________ (VERB ENDING IN "ING") in the countryside, and enjoy some of the famous ____________ (FOOD) and ____________ (BEVERAGE). But the next morning, I woke up to the train ____________ (OCCUPATION) announcing, "Now arriving in ____________ (EUROPEAN CITY)!" "____________ (EXCLAMATION)!" I yelled, as I woke the others. After talking with another passenger, we realized our mistake. We had ____________ (VERB (PAST TENSE)) tickets on a divided train. We didn't even know those existed! Divided trains split into two ____________ (ADJECTIVE) trains at one of the stations during the trip. We had chosen a sleeping ____________ (NOUN) in the wrong section of the train! Despite our mistake, our travel story had a(n) ____________ (EMOTION) ending. We got to explore a different city, go ____________ (VERB ENDING IN "ING") in a different countryside, and enjoy some amazing ____________ (FOOD) and ____________ (BEVERAGE). What an adventure!

ADJECTIVE
FIRST NAME (FRIEND)
ADJECTIVE
CLOTHING ITEM (PLURAL)
EXCLAMATION
ADJECTIVE
VERB ENDING IN “ING”
ADJECTIVE
COLOR
CLOTHING ITEM
BODY PART
TYPE OF BUSINESS
ADJECTIVE
NOUN
COLOR
MYSTICAL CREATURE
PLURAL NOUN
VERB

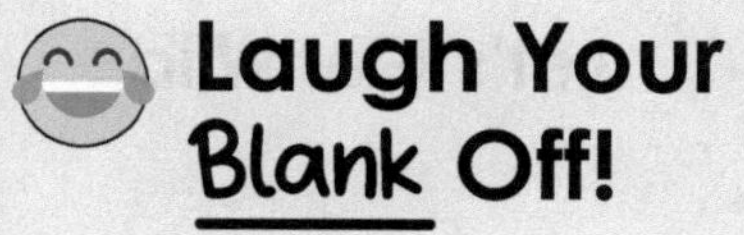

Travel Influencer

Hello you ______________ (ADJECTIVE) people! Thanks for coming back to my channel! ______________ (FIRST NAME (FRIEND)), here, with your next edition of "What I Bought on Vacation!" After I posted photos of me wearing my new ______________ (ADJECTIVE) ______________ (CLOTHING ITEM (PLURAL)) on the beach at St. Tropez, I got so many comments asking to see my favorite purchases from my trip there. ______________ (EXCLAMATION)! You guys are so ______________ (ADJECTIVE)! I just finished ______________ (VERB ENDING IN "ING") the video, so now I can show you my newest closet obsessions. Everything in St. Tropez is so ______________ (ADJECTIVE). So if you're looking for trending fashion, St. Tropez is your spot! First up: this ______________ (COLOR) ______________ (CLOTHING ITEM) that converts into a ______________ (BODY PART)-pack. 10 out of 10 stars! At the same ______________ (TYPE OF BUSINESS), I also bought this ______________ (ADJECTIVE) hat and ______________ (NOUN) necklace. I can't wait to wear them at my next yacht event! Next, and probably my favorite, is this ______________ (COLOR) bathing suit and cover-up set that makes me feel like a ______________ (MYSTICAL CREATURE). Need I say more? Then I saw this set of silk ______________ (PLURAL NOUN) out of the corner of my eye, and I couldn't ______________ (VERB). Thank you, St. Tropez, for the shopping spree of a lifetime!

PLURAL NOUN
VERB ENDING IN "ING"
OCCUPATION
FOOD
FOOD
VERB
EXCLAMATION
ANIMAL (PLURAL)
FIRST NAME (FRIEND)
ADJECTIVE
VERB
NUMBER
FIRST NAME (FRIEND)
FOOD
ANIMAL (PLURAL)
VERB
PLURAL NOUN
ADJECTIVE

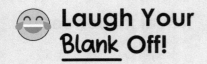

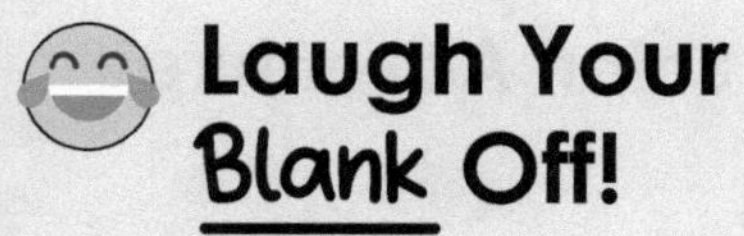

Let's Get Wild

Good morning, everyone! I'm James, your fearless tour guide. Are you ready to see some wild ____________ (PLURAL NOUN)? Today, we'll spend the day ____________ (VERB ENDING IN "ING") Serengeti National Park. The camp ____________ (OCCUPATION) has packed a tasty picnic for us, including ____________ (FOOD) soup, pasta with roasted ____________ (FOOD), and local fruit for dessert. We'll arrive before sunset and ____________ (VERB) under the stars tonight. ____________ (EXCLAMATION)! Look to your left everyone! Two minutes out of the gate and we've caught sight of some spotted ____________ (ANIMAL (PLURAL)) devouring their breakfast! ____________ (FIRST NAME (FRIEND)), stay in the vehicle! Do you see that? Those ____________ (ADJECTIVE) hippos look tame, but they're not friendly! Look at the massive baobab trees around us. Tourists are not the only ones who ____________ (VERB) them. Look in the branches! See those lions resting? Don't worry! Only ____________ (NUMBER) tourists have been eaten this season. We're probably be fine! ____________ (FIRST NAME (FRIEND)), put that ____________ (FOOD) away! ____________ (ANIMAL (PLURAL)) have the strongest sense of smell in the animal kingdom. We don't want a herd of them to ____________ (VERB) us. Hold tight to your ____________ (PLURAL NOUN) as you take pictures. The road is very ____________ (ADJECTIVE). Onward!

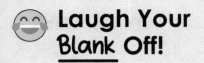

ADJECTIVE
VERB
VERB ENDING IN “ING”
VERB ENDING IN “ING”
ANIMAL (PLURAL)
PLURAL NOUN
ANIMAL (PLURAL)
COLOR
COLOR
VERB ENDING IN “ING”
ANIMAL (PLURAL)
SILLY SOUND
EXCLAMATION
ANIMAL
NOUN
VERB (PAST TENSE)
BODY PART

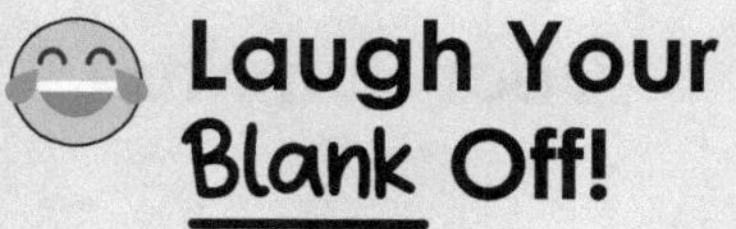

Safari Adventure

Dear Diary,

Wow! We returned from our trip to Africa last night, and it was

_____________! I want to _____________ everything down so I
ADJECTIVE VERB

never forget one second of our safari. We spent 10 days in

Tanzania _____________ through several world-famous parks, like
VERB ENDING IN "ING"

Mount Kilimanjaro National Park. We saw a pride of lions

_____________, a herd of _____________ grazing, tall giraffes
VERB ENDING IN "ING" ANIMAL (PLURAL)

eating _____________ off trees, ostriches running, _____________
PLURAL NOUN ANIMAL (PLURAL)

swinging in the trees, and graceful gazelles. We saw

_____________ and _____________ zebras bathing in rivers, black
COLOR COLOR

rhinos _____________ with their horns, huge _____________
VERB ENDING IN "ING" ANIMAL (PLURAL)

grunting and sleeping, and vultures searching for food. Every

night was an adventure as well. One night we heard a loud

"_____________!" right outside our tent. "_____________!"
SILLY SOUND EXCLAMATION

I yelled. "Is that a(n) _____________?!" Our safari guide came
ANIMAL

running. He said that it was just some monkeys trying to get our

_____________. He _____________ them off. I tried to sleep with
NOUN VERB (PAST TENSE)

one _____________ open after that. Would I safari again?
BODY PART

Absolutely! Adventure On!

DOG NAME
DOG BREED
FOOD
COUNTRY
ADJECTIVE
ADJECTIVE
ADJECTIVE
FOOD
PLURAL NOUN
NUMBER
ADJECTIVE
ANIMAL
SILLY NOISE
ADJECTIVE
VERB ENDING IN “ING”
NOUN

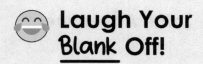

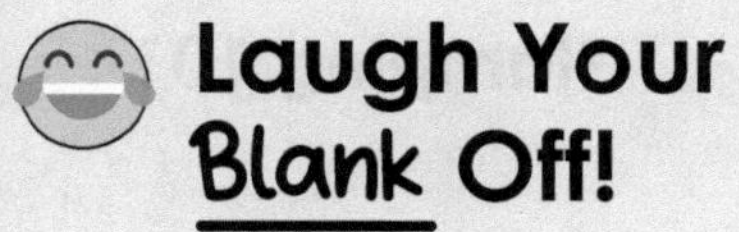

Dear Humans

Dear Humans - It's me, ____________ (DOG NAME). Remember me? Your beloved ____________ (DOG BREED) who you left for two weeks to explore Italy? How could you do this to me?! You know I love adventures, especially ones that involve ____________ (FOOD)! I thought we agreed after your last vacation trip to ____________ (COUNTRY), that you wouldn't vacation without me. I'll admit that I'm having a(n) ____________ (ADJECTIVE) time with grandma and grandpa at their house, but they don't have very good taste. They keep giving me ____________ (ADJECTIVE) food! Did you forget to tell them that I love ____________ (ADJECTIVE) bacon and juicy ____________ (FOOD)? I bring them ____________ (PLURAL NOUN) to throw so we can play fetch, but they only throw them about ______ (NUMBER) times before they get tired. I'm so ____________ (ADJECTIVE)! I haven't been to the ____________ (ANIMAL) park in forever! Remember, every human week is like 7 dog weeks! ____________ (SILLY NOISE)! That's dog for, "Come back now!" You've seen enough of ____________ (ADJECTIVE) Italy! Come see me! If you could see me now, you'd see that my tail is ____________ (VERB ENDING IN "ING") like crazy and I am definitely not sitting in Grandpa's favorite ____________ (NOUN).

Lots of love and dog kisses

NOUN
ADJECTIVE
ADJECTIVE
ADJECTIVE
NOUN
PLURAL NOUN
INSECT
NOUN
FURNITURE ITEM (PLURAL)
BEVERAGE
ADJECTIVE
NOUN
ADJECTIVE
BODY PART
ADJECTIVE
ADJECTIVE

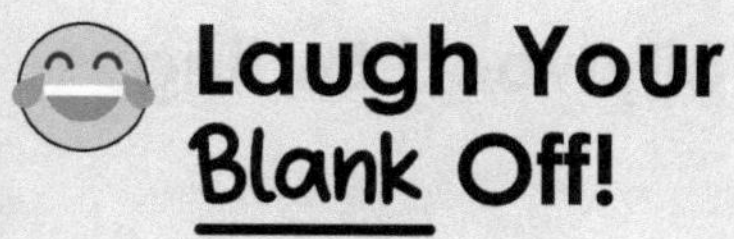

Glamping 101

Ready to get back to _____________ (NOUN) but not excited about roughing it? Try “glamping”! There are no _____________ (ADJECTIVE)-and-fast rules. You get to decide how much glamour to add to your camping experience. Here are some tips: 1 – Bring _____________ (ADJECTIVE) bedding. A(n) _____________ (ADJECTIVE) cot or a plush _____________ (NOUN) makes a good base. 2 – Add touches of home - Cute rugs or framed _____________ (PLURAL NOUN) will glamp up your décor. _____________ (INSECT) markets and _____________ (NOUN) sales are great places to find items that you won’t worry about ruining. 3 – Set up a “living room” – Kick back in comfort! Make sure you have plenty of _____________ (FURNITURE ITEM (PLURAL)), both big and small. Bonus if they have built-in cupholders, so you can keep your _____________ (BEVERAGE) handy. 4 – Light up your space – Strings of LED lights, _____________ (ADJECTIVE) candles and _____________ (NOUN)-powered lanterns will give your campsite a(n) _____________ (ADJECTIVE) glow. 5 – Set up stations - Create areas for _____________ (BODY PART)-washing with soap, _____________ (ADJECTIVE) water and clean towels. Or set up solar chargers for your _____________ (ADJECTIVE) devices. This is glamping afterall! You want to be able to take lots of photos of your gram-worthy getaway.

ADJECTIVE
VERB ENDING IN “ING”
BEVERAGE
FOOD
VERB (PAST TENSE)
ADJECTIVE
SILLY SOUND
NOUN
BODY PART
VERB (PAST TENSE)
VERB (PAST TENSE)
MALE FIRST NAME (ANYONE)
TYPE OF BUSINESS
OCCUPATION
VERB ENDING IN “ING”
CITY
TYPE OF MOVIE

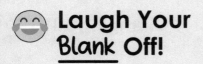

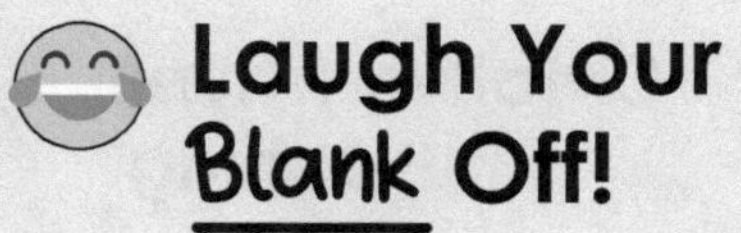

Hollywood Ending

How did we meet? It's a pretty ____________ (ADJECTIVE) story actually. It was a Friday night. I was ____________ (VERB ENDING IN "ING") on the couch with a glass of ____________ (BEVERAGE) and a bowl of ____________ (FOOD) watching a movie. I was supposed to go on a date with a pretty nice guy, but he ____________ (VERB (PAST TENSE)) on me at the last minute. Feeling ____________ (ADJECTIVE), I decided to check out ____________ (SILLY SOUND)-er. I matched with a few interesting guys and then went back to watching *The Billionaire and the* ____________ (NOUN). I wasn't expecting much, but my ____________ (BODY PART) flipped with excitement when my phone ____________ (VERB (PAST TENSE)) a few mintues later. One of my matches had ____________ (VERB (PAST TENSE)) me! ____________ (MALE FIRST NAME (ANYONE)) and I messaged all night. He asked me to be his date the next weekend for a friend's ____________ (TYPE OF BUSINESS) opening. He said he'd send his ____________ (OCCUPATION) to pick me up and we would catch a flight to the opening. I thought he was ____________ (VERB ENDING IN "ING"), but I went along with it. To my surprise, the opening was in ____________ (CITY)! I felt like I was starring in one of my favorite ____________ (TYPE OF MOVIE) movies. As you've probably guessed, we fell in love and got married. Just like in the movies!

EXCLAMATION
EMOTION
ADJECTIVE
VERB
VERB
ADJECTIVE
ADJECTIVE
COUNTRY
VERB ENDING IN "ING"
ADJECTIVE
NOUN
VERB
NUMBER
NOUN
VERB
NOUN
VERB ENDING IN "ING"
ADJECTIVE

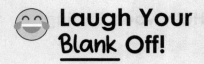

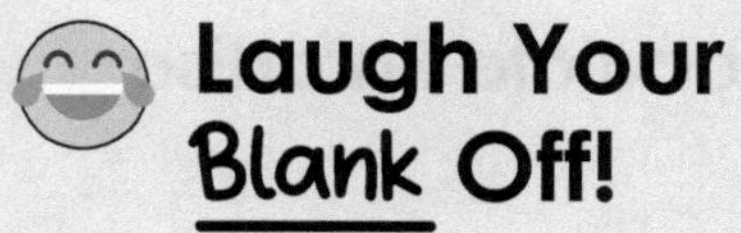

Creative Travel Planning

So, you and your partner finally have enough vacation time to take a trip together! ____________ (EXCLAMATION)! You're probably very ____________ (EMOTION) to plan your trip, but how do you decide where to go? Do you stay ____________ (ADJECTIVE) or travel out of the country? Do you prefer to fly or ____________ (VERB)? Do you want to ____________ (VERB) the great outdoors or try something ____________ (ADJECTIVE)? Maybe you like the idea of taking a(n) ____________ (ADJECTIVE) train trip through ____________ (COUNTRY), but your partner wants to go ____________ (VERB ENDING IN "ING") in Montana. How do you come up with a plan that you'll both like? It's time to get ____________ (ADJECTIVE)! Follow these steps to add ____________ (NOUN) to your vacation planning: 1 – You and your partner each think of three places you'd like to ____________ (VERB): one within a _______ (NUMBER)-hour drive, one in your country of residence, and one international location. Shhhh… Don't tell your partner your answers. 2 – Write your travel choices on small pieces of ____________ (NOUN) and ____________ (VERB) them up. 3 – You each put your choices into a ____________ (NOUN). 4 – Then take turns ____________ (VERB ENDING IN "ING") them out, one by one. The last one left will be your ____________ (ADJECTIVE) vacation destination! Enjoy your adventure!

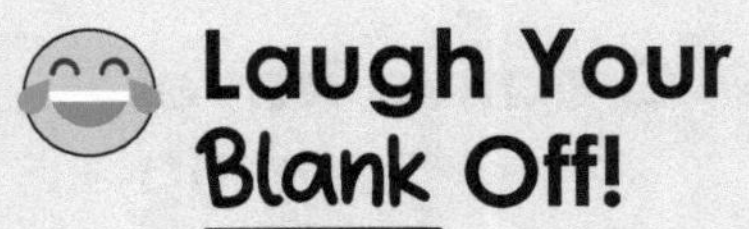

BODY PART
PLURAL NOUN
PLURAL NOUN
PLURAL NOUN
PLURAL NOUN
VERB
ADJECTIVE
VERB
ADJECTIVE
PLURAL NOUN
ADJECTIVE
FOOD
FOOD
FOOD
ADJECTIVE
PLURAL NOUN

Chocolate Paradise

Are you known for having the biggest sweet ____________ (BODY PART) around? Are you hopelessly addicted to chocolate? If so, imagine a land where *everything* is made of chocolate: the ____________ (PLURAL NOUN), trees, ____________ (PLURAL NOUN), animals, ____________ (PLURAL NOUN)… everything! All your wildest ____________ (PLURAL NOUN) about chocolate will come true here in Geneva, Switzerland. After you ____________ (VERB) at the airport, you're only minutes away from a chocoholic's dream: Switzerland's World of Cocoa. Every year, we're voted #1 on the list of ____________ (ADJECTIVE) European Attractions. You'll get to ____________ (VERB) our world-renowned chocolatiers and watch them whip up ____________ (ADJECTIVE) treats and decadent ____________ (PLURAL NOUN). Tour our state-of-the-art candy factory and take ____________ (ADJECTIVE) selfies surrounded by chocolate. Enjoy unlimited samples of your favorites, like double chocolate chip ____________ (FOOD), chocolate ____________ (FOOD) martinis, fudgy brownies, chocolate ____________ (FOOD) truffles, fountains of ____________ (ADJECTIVE) chocolate, and more! Learn the ____________ (PLURAL NOUN) to creating world-class chocolate and try making your own cocoa confections. Contact us today for sweet travel deals!

NOUN
EMOTION
CITY, STATE
CITY, STATE
NUMBER
NOUN
NUMBER
NUMBER
VERB ENDING IN “ING”
ADJECTIVE
BEVERAGE
VERB ENDING IN “ING”
NOUN
BODY PART
CITY
PLURAL NOUN
ADJECTIVE
ADJECTIVE
FIRST NAME (FRIEND)

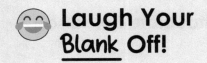

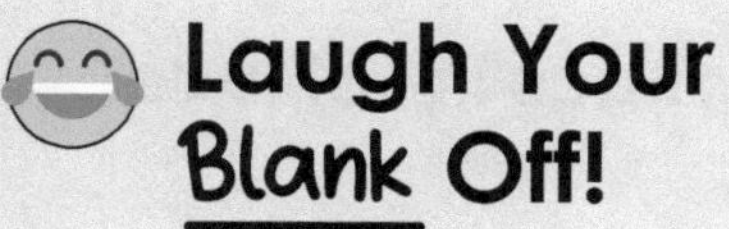

Flight From Hell

Dear _____________ (NOUN) Airlines,

I am a long-time customer, and I'm very _____________ (EMOTION) with your company! Last week, I traveled from _____________ (CITY), ___________ (STATE) to _____________ (CITY), ___________ (STATE) on flight A303. It was the worst flight I have ever taken! 1 — The flight was delayed for ______ (NUMBER) hours, so I missed my _____________ (NOUN) and had to wait another ______ (NUMBER) hours for a flight. 2 —There were ______ (NUMBER) _____________ (VERB ENDING IN "ING") babies on the plane. 3 — The air conditioning was ___________ (ADJECTIVE). 4 — They ran out of _____________ (BEVERAGE). 5 — I was stuck between two passengers who were _____________ (VERB ENDING IN "ING"). 6 — The pilot flew through a _____________ (NOUN) and the turbulence messed up my ___________ (BODY PART). 7 — The plane had a problem mid-air, so we made an unscheduled stop in _____________ (CITY). 8 — The overhead storage bins were too small for my _____________ (PLURAL NOUN). 9 — The flight attendants were _____________ (ADJECTIVE). 10 — Several passengers got really _____________ (ADJECTIVE). I expect to be compensated for my pain and suffering on this flight!

Sincerely,

____
FIRST NAME (FRIEND)

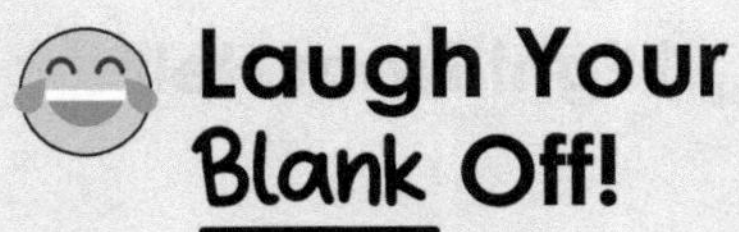

COUNTRY
VERB
EMOTION
NOUN
ADJECTIVE
EMOTION
ADJECTIVE
VERB ENDING IN “ING”
VERB ENDING IN “ING”
VERB ENDING IN “ING”
STATE
ADJECTIVE
VERB (PAST TENSE)
FOOD
VERB (PAST TENSE)
OCCUPATION

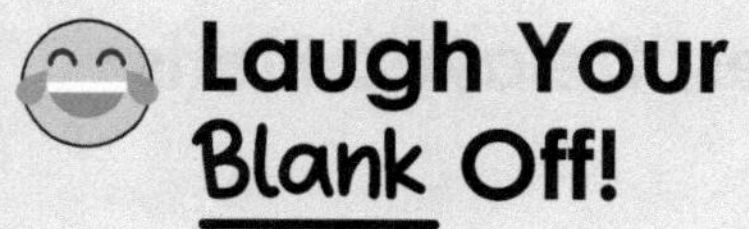

We've moved to ____________! Please update your address
COUNTRY
book with our new info. And please ____________ us too! If
VERB
you're ____________ that we moved here so suddenly, believe
EMOTION
us. We are too! What can we say? Our ____________ affair with
NOUN
this place started on our honeymoon. Planning a wedding is so stressful! So, after the ____________ day, we were
ADJECTIVE
____________ to relax and have fun. Jake wanted to do
EMOTION
something ____________ since we were ____________ at a
ADJECTIVE VERB ENDING IN "ING"
beautiful villa right on the beach. I thought he might suggest whale- ____________, fishing, or maybe ____________. But he
VERB ENDING IN "ING" VERB ENDING IN "ING"
suggested scuba diving! We both grew up on farms in upstate ____________, and we never visited the ocean as kids. But as
STATE
soon as we saw the ____________ sea and ____________ the
ADJECTIVE VERB (PAST TENSE)
salt air, we were hooked. We took scuba diving lessons, stuffed ourselves with delicious ____________ and ____________ on
FOOD VERB (PAST TENSE)
the beach as much as we could. As soon as we made it back home, we called a ____________ and put our house up for sale.
OCCUPATION
And the rest is history. Please visit us in this paradise!

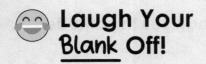

PLURAL NOUN
FEMALE FIRST NAME (FRIEND)
EMOTION
ADJECTIVE
ADJECTIVE
NOUN
EXCLAMATION
VERB ENDING IN “ING”
EXCLAMATION
COLOR
TYPE OF VEHICLE
ADJECTIVE
PLURAL NOUN
VERB (PAST TENSE)
VERB (PAST TENSE)
NOUN

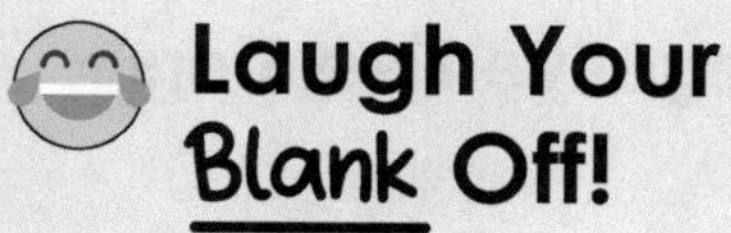

Best Delayed Plans

When I lived in Australia, I loved it when ____________ (PLURAL NOUN) came to visit. So, when my friend, ____________ (FEMALE FIRST NAME (FRIEND)) decided to spend her vacation with me, I was very ____________ (EMOTION) and told her I would pick her up at the airport. I have a(n) ____________ (ADJECTIVE) habit of being late for everything, but I was determined to be on time. I put the address for the Gold Coast Airport into my ____________ (ADJECTIVE) maps app and followed the directions. I looked at my ____________ (NOUN) as I arrived at the airport. "____________ (EXCLAMATION)!," I said to myself, "I'm early for a change!" I was ____________ (VERB ENDING IN "ING") outside the international arrivals area when I got a text from my friend. "I'm here! ____________ (EXCLAMATION)! Where are you?" "Me too!", I said. "I'm in a ____________ (COLOR) ____________ (TYPE OF VEHICLE), right outside of arrivals." "That's ____________ (ADJECTIVE)," she said. "I don't see you." That's when it hit me like a ton of ____________ (PLURAL NOUN). "Let me guess," I said. "You're at The Brisbane Airport. Not the Gold Coast Airport?" "Of course!" She replied. Two hours later, I ____________ (VERB (PAST TENSE)) at the correct airport, late as always. We just hugged and ____________ (VERB (PAST TENSE)). Next time, I will offer to pay for a ____________ (NOUN)!

NOUN
ADJECTIVE
EMOTION
ADJECTIVE
PLURAL NOUN
ADJECTIVE
VERB
VERB (PAST TENSE)
ADJECTIVE
VERB (PAST TENSE)
NUMBER
ADJECTIVE
SILLY NOISE
ADJECTIVE
VERB
ADJECTIVE
INSECT (PLURAL)
VERB

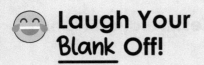

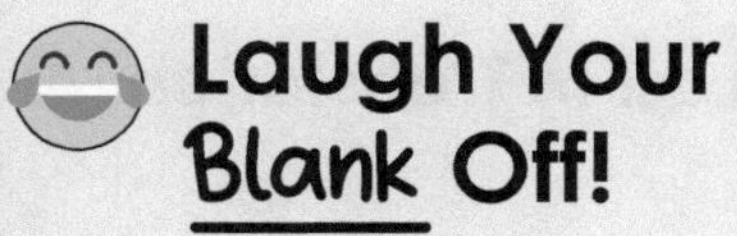

Negative Five Stars

Do not stay in this hotel! It is a total ____________ (NOUN)! My ____________ (ADJECTIVE) husband and I were ____________ (EMOTION) to explore Egypt on our honeymoon. We just didn't expect our first tour of ancient ruins to be at our hotel! We were fooled by their photos of ____________ (ADJECTIVE) views, charming ____________ (PLURAL NOUN), and ____________ (ADJECTIVE) dining. When we saw the "Hotel Closed, please go around the corner" sign at the entrance, we tried not to ____________ (VERB). As we turned the corner, we were ____________ (VERB (PAST TENSE)) by a(n) ____________ (ADJECTIVE) man. "Welcome to our temporary location," he said. He explained that a pipe had burst at the hotel we had booked and ____________ (VERB (PAST TENSE)) the whole building. It was after midnight, and we had been traveling for ____________ (NUMBER) hours, so we were too ____________ (ADJECTIVE) to ask many questions. ____________ (SILLY NOISE)! My husband started sneezing. There was dust everywhere! And it smelled ____________ (ADJECTIVE)! One look at our room, and we wanted to ____________ (VERB) away as fast as we could. The bed looked so ____________ (ADJECTIVE) and I saw ____________ (INSECT (PLURAL)) skittering across the floor! My husband and I didn't ____________ (VERB) a wink that night, but we did survive! First thing the next morning, we booked a new hotel. And it was wonderful!

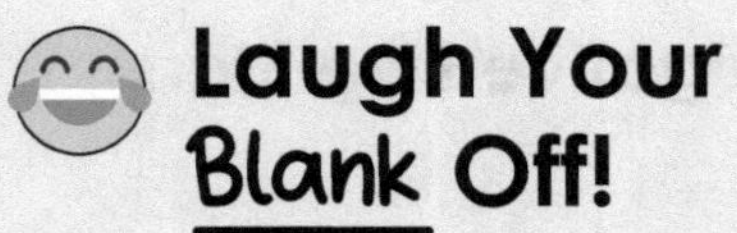

NOUN
NOUN
VERB ENDING IN “ING”
TYPE OF VEHICLE
NUMBER
ADJECTIVE
ADJECTIVE
ADJECTIVE
COLOR
ADJECTIVE
NOUN
NOUN
VERB
ADVERB ENDING IN “LY”
BODY PART
ADJECTIVE
NOUN
VERB (PAST TENSE)

Lost in Translation

I can't wait to tell you about my trip to Bolivia! You know it has been on my ____________ (NOUN) List for ages. I spent five ____________ (NOUN)-filled days and nights there ____________ (VERB ENDING IN "ING") the sights. I shared a ____________ (TYPE OF VEHICLE) with ____________ (NUMBER) other people, and we had a(n) ____________ (ADJECTIVE) tour guide named José. He took us through the desert and showed us ____________ (ADJECTIVE) sights, like ____________ (ADJECTIVE) lagoons where ____________ (COLOR) flamingos roam, a(n) ____________ (ADJECTIVE) ____________ (NOUN) graveyard, and some world-famous salt flats. One day, I was sitting in the front ____________ (NOUN) next to José. It was very hot in the vehicle. José didn't ____________ (VERB) much English, but I spoke Spanish ____________ (ADVERB ENDING IN "LY") — or so I thought. Just making small talk, I said, "Estoy caliente," which I thought meant, "I'm hot." But as soon as the words were out of my ____________ (BODY PART), he looked horrified. That's when a(n) ____________ (ADJECTIVE) Spanish speaker in the car spoke up: "You're telling him that you're hot for some romance. Is that what you meant to say?" Oops! Fortunately, my fellow passenger was able to explain my ____________ (NOUN) to José, and we all just ____________ (VERB (PAST TENSE)).

FEMALE FIRST NAME (FRIEND)
ADJECTIVE
CITY
ADJECTIVE
VERB
BEVERAGE
COLOR
ADJECTIVE
NOUN
ADJECTIVE
NOUN
NOUN
CLOTHING ITEM
EMOTION
VERB (PAST TENSE)
BODY PART
EXCLAMATION

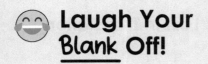

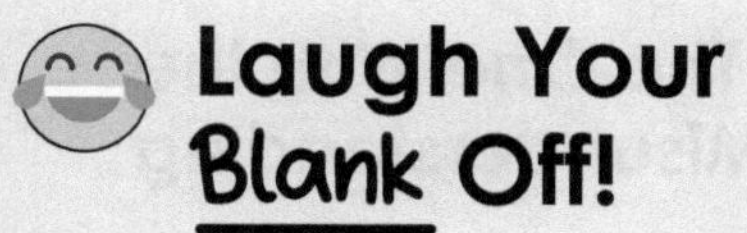

Plopping the Question

Speaking of creative proposals, have I ever told you how my friend, ____________ (FEMALE FIRST NAME (FRIEND)), got engaged? She and her fiancé had planned a(n) ____________ (ADJECTIVE) getaway to ____________ (CITY) to celebrate her birthday. He is very ____________ (ADJECTIVE), and he came up with an elaborate plan to ____________ (VERB) her. The first day of their trip, they were drinking ____________ (BEVERAGE) with brunch when the waiter came to their table and presented her with a rose. There was a note attached that said, “Roses are ____________ (COLOR), Violets are blue, you are ____________ (ADJECTIVE) and this your clue.” It was the first clue in a(n) ____________ (NOUN) hunt that led to a sailboat. She was ____________ (ADJECTIVE) and having ____________ (NOUN), but she still had no idea what he was up to. That’s when his plan went a little overboard. Because the engagement ____________ (NOUN) fell out of his ____________ (CLOTHING ITEM) and dropped into the water. She didn’t realize what had happened, so she was very ____________ (EMOTION) when he ____________ (VERB (PAST TENSE)) in the water. Fortunately, he was able to grab the jewelry box before it sank out of reach. Then, completely soaked, he got down on one ____________ (BODY PART) and asked her to marry him. ____________ (EXCLAMATION)! She said, “Yes! Of course I will.” They had such a fun time that they decided to go sailing on their honeymoon.

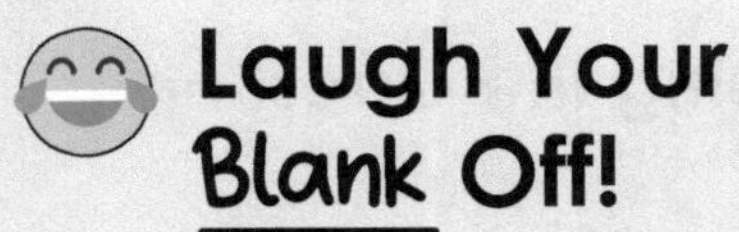

The One With the Misunderstanding

ADJECTIVE
VERB
NOUN
SILLY SOUND
ADJECTIVE
NOUN
NUMBER
NOUN
OCCUPATION
NUMBER
NOUN
FURNITURE ITEM
ADJECTIVE
ADJECTIVE
CLOTHING ITEM (PLURAL)
EXCLAMATION
CLOTHING ITEM

The One With the Misunderstanding

I recently took a business trip to Hong Kong. After a(n) __________ (ADJECTIVE) day of meetings, I really needed to __________ (VERB) and destress, so I decided to treat myself to a nice __________ (NOUN). I looked up spas on __________ (SILLY SOUND). I don't speak much Chinese, but a place called The __________ (ADJECTIVE) __________ (NOUN) had __________ (NUMBER) 5-star reviews, so I decided to try it. With its big, flashing __________ (NOUN) in the window, the spa was hard to miss! The __________ (OCCUPATION) who greeted me did not speak much English, so I just looked at the list of services and pointed at # ______ (NUMBER). She smiled and led me into a __________ (NOUN)-lit room with a massage __________ (FURNITURE ITEM) in it. When she left, I took off my clothes and wrapped myself in a(n) __________ (ADJECTIVE) towel. Soon, there was a knock at the door and a(n) __________ (ADJECTIVE) woman entered. She was wearing high-heeled __________ (CLOTHING ITEM (PLURAL)) and not much else! __________ (EXCLAMATION)! I thought to myself. Wrong kind of massage. I got dressed so fast, I left wearing my __________ (CLOTHING ITEM) backwards. It wasn't a relaxing experience, but it sure was funny!

VERB ENDING IN "ING"
ADJECTIVE
CITY
EMOTION
NUMBER
ADJECTIVE
VERB
NOUN
ADJECTIVE
VERB (PAST TENSE)
VERB (PAST TENSE)
NOUN
OCCUPATION (PLURAL)
VERB
PLURAL NOUN
COLOR
INSECT (PLURAL)

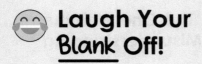

Beware of Gorilla

This is YNN with ____________ (VERB ENDING IN “ING”) news! Gertrude, the ____________ (ADJECTIVE) gorilla at the ____________ (CITY) Zoo, has escaped! Many zoo visitors were ____________ (EMOTION) today after traveling from near and far to visit Gertrude on her birthday. She turned ____________ (NUMBER) today and appears to have planned a special celebration. Gertrude is not ____________ (ADJECTIVE), so please try to stay calm if you ____________ (VERB) her. A zoo spokesperson said she is quite friendly, but warned residents: “Do not try to take a ____________ (NOUN) with her!” Gertrude escaped early this morning and has made herself ____________ (ADJECTIVE) at the Downtown Condominiums complex. Gertrude first entered Unit 4F, where she ____________ (VERB (PAST TENSE)) the fridge and ____________ (VERB (PAST TENSE)) on the walls. She then broke into a unit on the top floor and threw a ____________ (NOUN) through the window. Fortunately, nobody was hurt! City ____________ (OCCUPATION (PLURAL)) are advising residents to lock their doors and windows and ____________ (VERB) indoors. Major ____________ (PLURAL NOUN) will be closed until Gertrude is safely recaptured. Officials say they will try using her birthday cake to lure Gertrude out. “____________ (COLOR) icing with bananas and ____________ (INSECT (PLURAL)) is her favorite!”

ADJECTIVE
OCCUPATION
FOOD
STATE
NUMBER
VERB ENDING IN "ING"
NOUN
VEGETABLE
BEVERAGE
ADJECTIVE
ADJECTIVE
MALE FIRST NAME (ANYONE)
NUMBER
NOUN
ADJECTIVE
BODY PART
ADJECTIVE

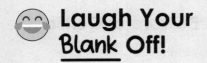

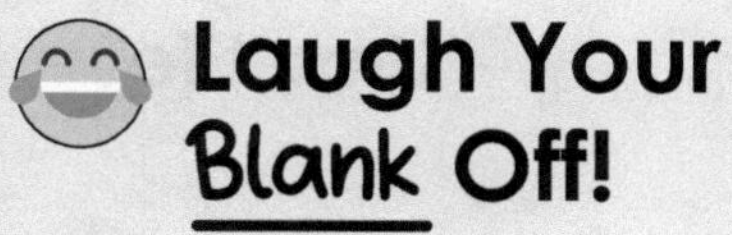

Surprise Guest

It's not unusual for a bachelor party to have a "surprise guest." You know, like when a(n) ____________ (ADJECTIVE) entertainer shows up in a(n) ____________ (OCCUPATION) uniform, or maybe pops out of a ____________ (FOOD)? But my friend Bob's party was different. We rented a house in the mountains of ____________ (STATE) with enough room for ____________ (NUMBER) guys. The first night, we were all ____________ (VERB ENDING IN "ING") out in the backyard. Some guys were floating in the ____________ (NOUN), and others were playing ____________ (VEGETABLE)-hole and ____________ (BEVERAGE) Pong. We were blasting music, when the doorbell rang. Bob answered the door and there was a(n) ____________ (ADJECTIVE) guy standing there. He said, "Hi! I'm here for Bob's party." Bob looked ____________ (ADJECTIVE) and asked, "Do I know you?" "Not yet!," the guy said, "I'm ____________ (MALE FIRST NAME (ANYONE)) ____________ (NUMBER) @gmail.com." Turns out, his email address was almost exactly the same as one of Bob's other friends. "I figured it was a ____________ (NOUN)," he said. "But the party sounded ____________ (ADJECTIVE), so here I am!" Bob started laughing his ____________ (BODY PART) off! Bob's surprise guest was a(n) ____________ (ADJECTIVE) guy. He fit in so well that he's coming to the wedding too!

NUMBER
ADJECTIVE
NOUN
OCCUPATION (PLURAL)
ADJECTIVE
CITY
ADJECTIVE
COUNTRY
CLOTHING ITEM (PLURAL)
CLOTHING ITEM (PLURAL)
BEVERAGE
FOOD
EMOTION
FOOD
TYPE OF BUSINESS
ADJECTIVE
NOUN
VERB ENDING IN "ING"

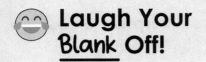

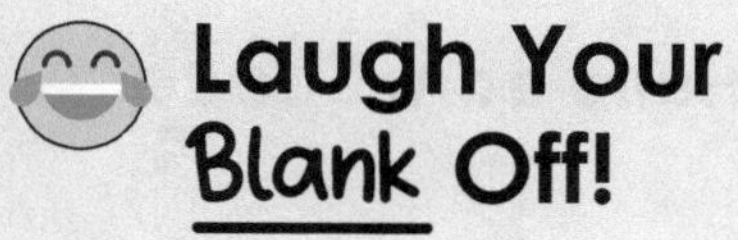

Limo Life

As a limousine driver for the past ______ (NUMBER) years, I have driven my share of ____________ (ADJECTIVE) clients, including ____________ (NOUN) stars, famous ____________ (OCCUPATION (PLURAL)), ____________ (ADJECTIVE) celebrities… you name it. International clients are always interesting. Every time I pick up a client at ____________ (CITY) International Airport, I know it will be someone ____________ (ADJECTIVE). I've even driven royalty! That's right, the Prince of ____________ (COUNTRY) once hired me. You couldn't tell by looking at him, dressed in ripped ____________ (CLOTHING ITEM (PLURAL)) and high-top ____________ (CLOTHING ITEM (PLURAL)). But "His Highness," as his bodyguard referred to him, was used to getting the royal treatment. My client had requested that I stock the cooler with expensive ____________ (BEVERAGE) and gourmet ____________ (FOOD). So, I was ____________ (EMOTION) when he asked me to go through the drive-through at ____________ (FOOD) King. The bodyguard asked me to make another stop on the way to the luxury ____________ (TYPE OF BUSINESS) where he'd be staying. When I did, two ____________ (ADJECTIVE) women got into the limo and the bodyguard moved up front with me. I raised the privacy screen, and they turned the ____________ (NOUN) up very loud, but I could still hear a lot of ____________ (VERB ENDING IN "ING") in the back. I'm happy to report that he tipped me a princely sum.

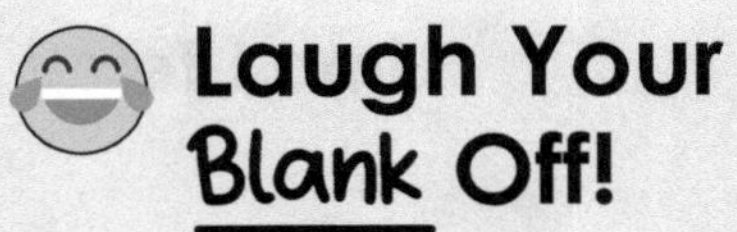

Hello from Space

FIRST NAME (FRIEND)
NUMBER
OCCUPATION
VERB
VERB
PLANET
VERB ENDING IN "ING"
ADJECTIVE
NUMBER
ANIMAL (PLURAL)
FOOD
FOOD
BEVERAGE
NOUN
EMOTION
ADJECTIVE
PLANET
VERB ENDING IN "ING"

Hello from Space

Dear ____________,
FIRST NAME (FRIEND)

It's day ____________ here in space. Being a(n) ____________
NUMBER / OCCUPATION

has always been my dream job. But I still ____________ every
VERB

day that we're apart. Here are some updates since yesterday: I wasn't able to ____________ last night. There was some drama,
VERB

apparently, between the Sun and ____________ that triggered a
PLANET

spacestorm. Our rocket kept ____________ up and down like a
VERB ENDING IN "ING"

toy on the ocean. It's times like these that I really miss our

____________ bed with ____________ fluffy pillows. Are the
ADJECTIVE / NUMBER

____________ keeping you company at night? We finally finished
ANIMAL (PLURAL)

our ____________ this morning. So, tomorrow, we will open a box
FOOD

of ____________ cereal and powdered ____________ for
FOOD / BEVERAGE

breakfast. What a ____________! My last spacewalk is tomorrow,
NOUN

and I am very ____________ about that! I will be repairing the
EMOTION

rocket booster, but don't worry! It will be ____________! And then,
ADJECTIVE

we will start our journey back to ____________. Before you know
PLANET

it, we'll be reunited, and you will get to hear my loud

____________ again every night.
VERB ENDING IN "ING"

Love you to infinity,

Your Space Explorer

Thank you for trying us out

A favor please 

Would you take a quick minute to leave us a rating/review on Amazon? It makes a *HUGE* difference and we would really appreciate it!

More fun from JBC Story Press

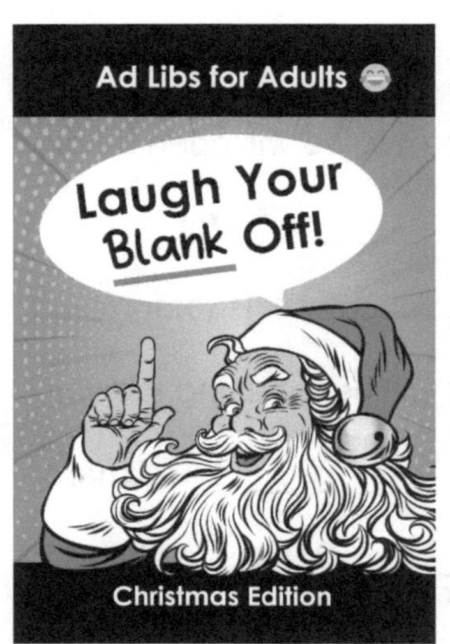

To see more, visit this link **http://amazon.com/author/jbcstory** or scan this code!

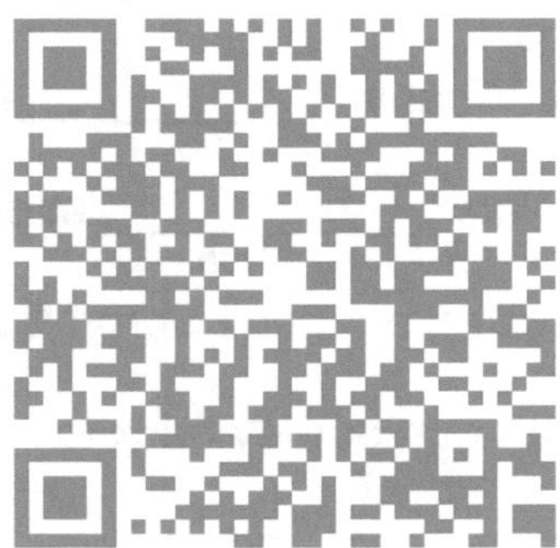

Do you like freebies?
Please send email to
info@jbcempowerpress.com
and we'll send you free funny stuff!

Made in United States
Troutdale, OR
11/01/2023

14218706R00030